Remembering Baby Ryan

Written by:
THE CARSON FAMILY

Illustrated by:
ISABELLA BELLIZZI

Cover Illustration by:
KAITLYNN CARSON

Remembering Baby Ryan

Copyright © 2019 by The Carson Family. All rights reserved.

No rights claimed for public domain material, all rights reserved.
No parts of this publication may be reproduced, stored in any retrieval system,
or transmitted in any form or by any means, electronic, mechanical, recording,
or otherwise, without the prior written permission of the author.
Violations may be subject to civil or criminal penalties.

ISBN:
978-1-63308-522-0 (paperback)
978-1-63308-523-7 (ebook)

Cover and Interior Design by *R'tor John D. Maghuyop*
Illustrated by *Isabella Bellizzi*
Cover Illustration by *Kaitlynn Carson*

CHALFANT ECKERT
PUBLISHING

1028 S Bishop Avenue, Dept. 178
Rolla, MO 65401

Printed in United States of America

Remembering Baby Ryan

Written by:
THE CARSON FAMILY

Illustrated by:
ISABELLA BELLIZZI

Cover Illustration by:
KAITLYNN CARSON

*The Carson Family
would like to thank
Johns Hopkins Hospital
for their efforts.*

This is the story

Of a baby boy

Who brought his family

Love and joy

A life so short

A child so small

A story so moving

It has touched us all

The little boy's name

Is Baby Ryan

Though he was tiny

He had the heart of a lion

Very shortly

After Ryan was born

The family received news

That had them torn

Baby Ryan

Just twelve days old

Had a tumor in his brain

The doctors told

The family could not believe

What was diagnosed

It was news that

They feared the most

Baby Ryan fought

Until he could fight no more

His time on Earth was short

But his impact couldn't be ignored

What Ryan and his family

Have endured

Is nothing short of heartbreaking

We must find a cure

Though his limited days with us

Were physically painful

Baby Ryan

Is now an angel

Now in heaven

He feels no pain

Memories of Baby Ryan

Will always remain

This is not where

Baby Ryan's story ends

This is only the beginning

We will be with him again

Baby Ryan will forever

Be in our hearts

When we see him again

Our real story will start

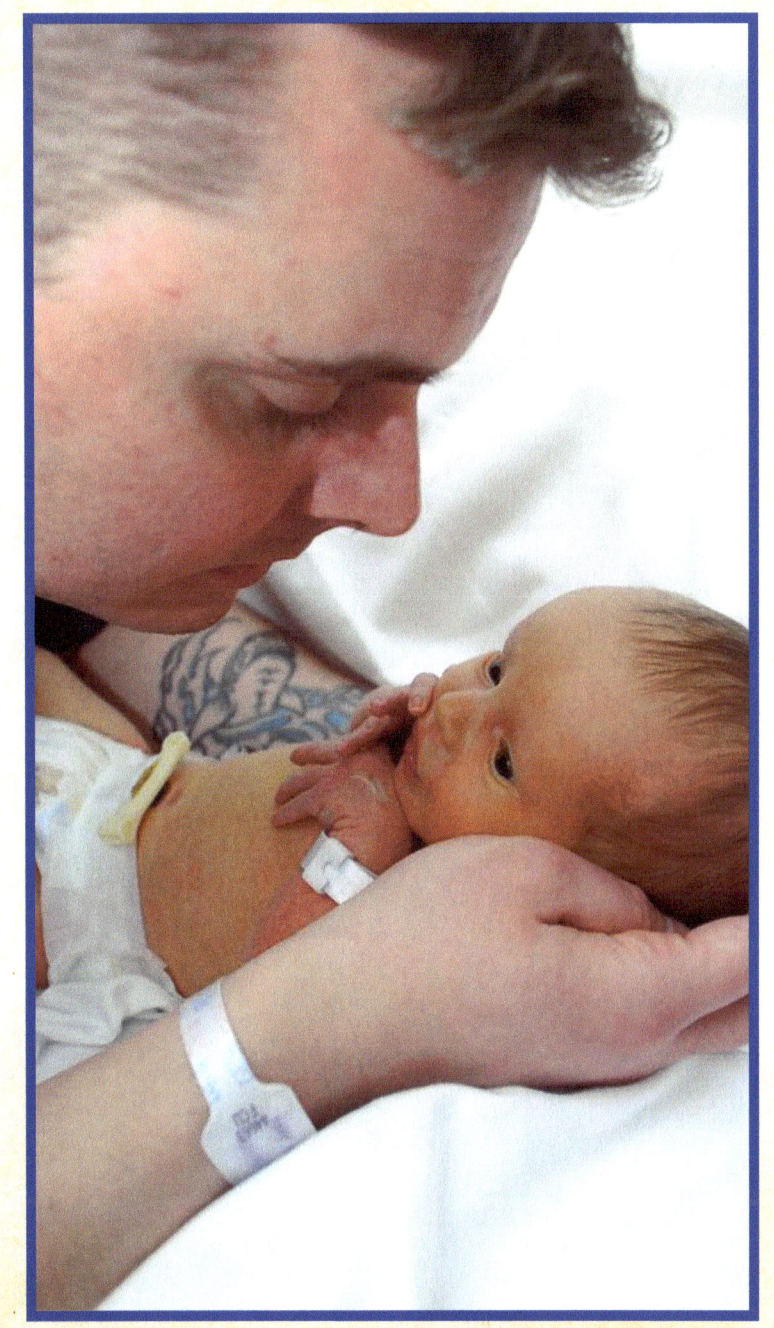

www.ingramcontent.com/pod-product-compliance
Lightning Source LLC
Chambersburg PA
CBHW042028150426
43198CB00002B/96